Parts of Speech

by Tina Dubuque

TABLE OF CONTENTS

PAGE	TITLE	CONCEPTS AND SKILLS
1	So Many Nouns, So Little Time	Proper & Common Nouns
2	Seeing Isn't Always Believing	Concrete & Abstract Nouns
3	Name That Group	Collective Nouns
4	One or More?	Singular & Plural Nouns
5	A Bit More Information	Nouns & Appositives
6	A Noun by Any Other Name	Pronouns
7	Jumpin' Java	Action & Linking Verbs
8	Lending a Helping Hand	Main & Helping Verbs
9	Silly Sentences	Principal Parts of Verbs
10	Yesterday, Today, and Tomorrow	Simple Verb Tense
11	Just Perfect!	Perfect Verb Tense
12	A New Home	Irregular Verbs
13	Making Progress	Progressive Verb Tense
14	Look for an Object	Transitive & Intransitive Verbs
15	A Change of Voice	Active vs. Passive Voice
16	Putting It All Together	Conjunctions
17	The More, the Merrier!	Conjunctions & Compounds
18	Say It with Feeling	Interjections
19	Describe It to Me	Adjectives
20	Typical Terms	Adjectives
21	Children's Stories	Possessive Adjectives
22	Tricky Terms	Possessive Adjectives
23	"Scent"sational	Adverbs
24	Adverb Additions	Adverbs
25	Designating Degree	Degrees of Comparison
26	Up, Down, and All Around	Prepositions
27	Think of a Word	Parts of Speech Review
28	Think of a Word (continued)	Parts of Speech Review

The activities in this book provide students with fundamental knowledge of the basic parts of speech. The pages clearly define and explain the roles of each of the eight parts of speech. A wide variety of activities requires students to identify and use the parts of speech correctly. Pages 27 and 28 contain a humorous, motivational review that may be used to assess students' understanding of parts of speech.

© 1998 McDONALD PUBLISHING CO.

Answers

Page 1
1. uniform, common
   game, common
2. Jennifer, proper
   present, common
   birthday, common
3. exhibit, common
   Miller Museum, proper
4. Thomas Jefferson, proper
   report, common
5. test, common
   French, proper
6. music, common
   Mozart, proper
   piano, common
7. cookies, common
   party, common
8. Ralph, proper
   car, common

Page 2
1. Brendan, proper, concrete
   friends, common, concrete
2. Mark, proper, concrete
   Luke, proper, concrete
   bicycles, common, concrete
3. group, common, concrete
   trail, common, concrete
   hours, common, abstract
4. wind, common, concrete
   leaves, common, concrete
   branches, common, concrete
5. boys, common, concrete
   adventure, common, abstract
6. Dan, proper, concrete
   tracks, common, concrete
   trail, common, concrete
7. tracks, common, concrete
   human, common, concrete
   bear, common, concrete
8. Brendan, proper, concrete
   Mark, proper, concrete
   tracks, common, concrete
   creature, common, concrete
9. boys, common, concrete
   time, common, abstract

Page 3
1. F   6. H
2. J   7. A
3. I   8. C
4. E   9. G
5. D   10. B

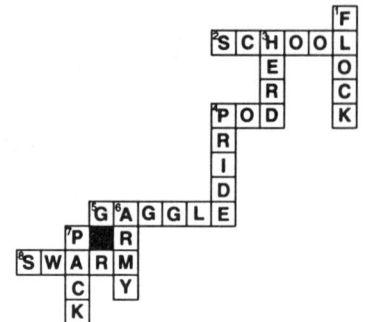

Page 4
1. dogs   9. children
2. chimneys   10. potatoes
3. wishes   11. knives
4. loaves   12. axes
5. boxes   13. benches
6. bushes   14. pennies
7. states   15. radios
8. ranches

Page 5
Answers will vary. Be sure students punctuate correctly.

Page 6
Paragraph 1: You, I, them, us, We, them, we
Paragraph 2: she, She, I (think), she
Paragraph 3: I (miss), you, I (am), you, me

Page 7
1. opened, A   9. are, L
2. roasts, A   10. offers, A
3. are, L   11. enjoyed, A
4. like, A   12. is, L
5. serve, A   13. perform, A
6. bakes, A   14. seems, L
7. holds, A   15. attracts, A
8. eat, A   16. love, A

Page 8
1. (is) seeking   9. (are) selling
2. (are) needed   10. (will) enjoy
3. (must) find   11. (is) offering
4. (should) apply   12. (can) establish
5. (may) expand   13. (is) scheduling
6. (is) looking   14. (will) need
7. (must) hire   15. (will) offer
8. (is) expanding

Page 9
1. talk, talking, talked
2. running, ran, run
3. ride, rode, ridden
4. want, wanting, wanted
5. bake, baking, baked

Remaining sentences will vary. Be sure principal parts of verbs are formed correctly.

Page 10
1. borrowed
2. likes, washes
3. went, was
4. was
5. told
6. promised
7. caught
8. needed
9. talked, will remember
10. says, guess

Students' sentences will vary.

Page 11
1. has returned
2. had heard
3. had made
4. had anticipated
5. will have spent
6. had gone
7. had dropped
8. will have been
9. had been

Page 12
was, had been, approached, prepared, became, was, arrived, began, saw, were, had dreaded, was, made, helped, joined, began, thought, had, decided

Page 13
1. (are, am, is) talking
   (were, was) talking
   will be talking
   (have, has) been talking
   had been talking
   will have been talking
2. (are, am, is) writing
   (were, was) writing
   will be writing
   (have, has) been writing
   had been writing
   will have been writing
3. (are, am, is) swimming
   (were, was) swimming
   will be swimming
   (have, has) been swimming
   had been swimming
   will have been swimming

Students' speeches will vary but should use the correct progressive verb tenses.

Page 14
1. threw—T, (passes)
2. slept—I
3. move—T, (box)
4. called—T, (name)
5. climbed—I
6. walked—I
7. gathered—I
8. broke—T, (china)
9. hears—T, (words)
10. gave—T, (show)
11. increased—I

Page 15
1. P
2. A
3. A
4. P
5. A

Paragraphs may vary slightly.

The seventh grade class took a field trip to the zoo. One of the school's bus drivers drove the students. The students toured the Children's Zoo. There they saw a newborn chimpanzee. A zookeeper was feeding the chimpanzee a bottle. The zookeeper asked the students to suggest names for the chimp. The zookeeper told the students that the student with the best suggestion would win a membership to the zoo.

Page 16
Conjunctions may vary slightly.
1. and
2. but
3. either, or
4. if
5. although
6. unless
7. Both, and
8. since
9. than
10. but
11. before

Page 17
1. Luke, Julie, (and) Laura—CS
2. would see a science-fiction movie (and) eat pizza afterward—CP
3. Julie (and) Laura—CS
4. Laura (and) Luke; called their mothers for permission (and) said they would be home by 9 P.M.—B
5. Karen (and) Mike—CS
6. decided to join the group at the movie (but) knew they had to call home first—CP
7. gave them permission (and) told them to have fun—CP

8. drove in Luke's car (and) stopped at the bank for money first—CP
9. arrived at the theater (and) learned that the science-fiction blockbuster was sold out—CP
10. Luke (and) Laura; decided to see an action-adventure movie instead (and) bought two sodas and a large popcorn to share—B
11. Mike, Karen, (and) Julie; went on to dinner (and) said they'd pick up the others after the movie—B
12. Laura (and) Luke; enjoyed the movie (and) munched on their snacks—B

Page 18
Interjections for 1-6 will vary but should be appropriate for the situations.
Sentences for 7-11 will vary but should be appropriate following the interjections.
12. C
13. D
14. B
15. A

Page 19
1. a new Italian (cookbook)
2. a pasta (recipe), last (night)
3. chicken (cannelloni), a cream (sauce)
4. leftover (chicken), a previous (meal)
5. a long (time), ten (minutes)
6. The Mediterranean (dish), heavy (cream), olive (oil)
7. fantastic (spaghetti)
8. delicious (taste)
9. secret (recipe)
10. easy (parts)
11. store-bought (noodles)
12. fresh (vegetables)
13. mysterious (sauce)
14. sweet, spicy (taste)
15. amazing (skill)

Page 20
Answers and paragraphs will vary.

Page 21
Note that some sources refer to possessive adjectives as possessive nouns.
1. seeds' magic
2. a harp's melody
3. a giant's wrath
4. a vine's growth
5. a goose's eggs
"Jack and the Beanstalk"
6. a mirror's honesty
7. a prince's kiss
8. small men's work
9. a queen's trick
10. some apples' poison
"Snow White and the Seven Dwarfs"
11. a clock's chime
12. a prince's search
13. sisters' taunting
14. a wand's magic
15. mice's transformation
"Cinderella"
Remaining answers will vary.

Page 22
1. It's
2. its
3. it's
4. It's
5. its
6. its
7. its
8. Sentences will vary.
9. There
10. They're
11. They're
12. their
13. there
14. there
15. They're
16. there
17. their

Page 23
1. appropriately (suit)
2. very (strong)
3. easily (smell)
4. instantly (alerts)
5. very (advanced)
6. extremely (sensitive)
7. even (detect)
8. heavily (rely)
9. often (leave)
10. most (important)
11. much (less), less (sharpened)
12. greatly (improve)

Page 24
Adverbs will vary.

Page 25
1. bad, worst
2. smoothly, more smoothly
3. more often, most often
4. skillfully, most skillfully
5. tall, taller
Paragraphs will vary but should include the degrees of comparison specified.

Page 26
Sentences 1 and 2 will vary.
3. thin ice
4. a lake
5. your hat
6. her eyes
7. the bag
Paragraphs will vary.

Pages 27 & 28
Answers will vary but should match the required parts of speech.

So Many Nouns, So Little Time

A **noun** is a word that names a person, place, thing, or idea. A **common noun** names any person, place, thing, or idea. A **proper noun** names a specific person, place, or thing. Proper nouns are capitalized.

<u>common nouns</u>   <u>proper nouns</u>
man   city   George   Washington, D.C.

Find and circle the nouns in the following "to do" list. Write each noun in the first column. Then, in the second column, label each noun as common or proper.

<u>Things to Do</u>

1. Wash uniform for game.

2. Buy Jennifer a present for her birthday.

3. See exhibit at Miller Museum.

4. Research Thomas Jefferson for report.

5. Study for test in French.

6. Practice music by Mozart on the piano.

7. Bake cookies for party.

8. Call Ralph about fixing car.

Noun	Type
1.	
2.	
3.	
4.	
5.	
6.	
7.	
8.	

Name _____   Concrete & Abstract Nouns

Seeing Isn't Always Believing

A **concrete noun** names something you can see, hear, smell, taste, or touch. An **abstract noun** names ideas, feelings, and characteristics such as bravery, love, or happiness.

Read each of the following sentences. In the first column, write the nouns from each sentence. In the next column, label each noun as common or proper. Finally, in the third column, write whether each noun is abstract or concrete.

Noun	Common or Proper	Concrete or Abstract
Saturday	*proper*	*abstract*
hikers	*common*	*concrete*
entrance	*common*	*concrete*

Example:
Last Saturday several hikers met at the park's entrance.

1. Brendan had suggested the four friends meet.

2. Mark and Luke rode up on their bicycles.

3. The group walked the rugged trail for three hours.

4. The wind rustled the leaves and tree branches.

5. The boys enjoyed their adventure.

6. Dan noticed some very large tracks off the trail.

7. The tracks were too large to belong to any human or bear.

8. Brendan and Mark were certain the tracks belonged to a Bigfoot-like creature.

9. The other boys nervously decided it was time to leave.

©1998 McDONALD PUBLISHING CO.   PARTS OF SPEECH

Name _____   Collective Nouns

Name That Group

A **collective noun** is a word that names a group of persons, animals, or things. For example, the collective noun *team* refers to a group of players.

Write letters in the blanks to match each collective noun with its corresponding noun.

1. ____ class
2. ____ crew
3. ____ congregation
4. ____ army
5. ____ audience
6. ____ faculty
7. ____ cast
8. ____ choir
9. ____ band
10. ____ electorate

A. actors
B. voters
C. singers
D. viewers
E. soldiers
F. students
G. musicians
H. teachers
I. worshipers
J. astronauts

Each puzzle clue below is the name of a type of animal. To complete the puzzle, write the collective noun that names a group of each type of animal.

Across
2. fish
4. whale
5. goose
8. bee

Down
1. sheep
3. cow
4. lion
6. ant
7. wolf

©1998 McDONALD PUBLISHING CO.   3   PARTS OF SPEECH

Name _____   Singular & Plural Nouns

One or More?

A **singular noun** names one person, place, thing, or idea. A **plural noun** names more than one person, place, thing, or idea. Use the guide below to form the plural of most nouns. Note that many nouns do not follow the rules.

Type of Noun	To Make It Plural	Example
most nouns	Add *s*.	tree — trees
nouns ending in *s, x, z, sh,* or *ch*	Add *es*.	branch — branches
nouns ending in *y* after a consonant	Change *y* to *i* and add *es*.	baby — babies
nouns ending in *y* after a vowel	Add *s*.	day — days
nouns ending in *o* after a consonant	Add *es*.	tomato — tomatoes
nouns ending in *o* after a vowel	Add *s*.	patio — patios
nouns ending in *f* or *fe*	Change *f* or *fe* to *v* and add *es*.	wolf — wolves

Some nouns keep the same form in the singular and the plural.   deer — deer

Some nouns form the plural with a new word.   woman — women

Write the plural of each noun to complete the sentences.

(dog)   1. Our neighbors keep their three _____ outside.

(chimney) 2. We hired a company to clean our _____.

(wish)   3. How many _____ did you make when you blew out the candles?

(loaf)   4. I bought two fresh _____ of bread at the bakery.

(box)   5. The gifts are wrapped in beautiful _____.

(bush)   6. Last winter, birds built a nest in one of our many _____.

(state)   7. Our new neighbors have lived in _____ all over the country.

(ranch)   8. Mara's family owns several cattle _____ in California.

(child)   9. Two more _____ will be in our class next year.

(potato) 10. The home economics teacher published a cookbook filled with our recipes for cooking _____.

(knife)   11. Please be sure to put those _____ in the drawer.

(ax)   12. My neighbor broke two _____ while chopping wood.

(bench)   13. We'll put those _____ on the playground.

(penny)   14. When I looked into my piggy bank, the only thing I saw was a large pile of _____.

(radio)   15. No _____ are allowed in that library.

A Bit More Information

An **appositive** is a word or phrase that follows a noun and provides more information about the noun.
My dog, Spot, is a dalmatian.

Use commas to set off an appositive that adds extra information to a sentence.
Lassie, a collie, was a famous dog.

Do not use commas with appositives that add essential information to a sentence. The following example is not set off by commas. It tells specifically which dog was on television.
The dog Rin-Tin-Tin was also on television.

Rewrite the following sentences, using appositives to add information about the underlined nouns. Punctuate correctly.

1. Seana wrote a letter about her new dog.
   _____

2. Her family purchased the dog in Houston last summer.
   _____
   _____

3. They chose the breed after doing some library research.
   _____
   _____

4. One book was especially helpful to them.
   _____
   _____

5. They took their dog to a well-known trainer.
   _____

6. He has learned a new trick.
   _____

7. He has also stopped one of his troublesome behaviors.
   _____
   _____

A Noun by Any Other Name

A **pronoun** is a word that takes the place of a noun. Like nouns, pronouns refer to people, places, things, and ideas. The form that a pronoun takes depends on its use in the sentence. Subject pronouns are used as subjects. Object pronouns are used as direct objects, indirect objects, and objects of prepositions. Possessive pronouns indicate possession or ownership.

Subject Pronouns		Object Pronouns		Possessive Pronouns	
Singular	Plural	Singular	Plural	Singular	Plural
I	we	me	us	mine	ours
you	you	you	you	yours	yours
he, she, it	they	him, her, it	them	his, hers, its	theirs

Without pronouns, nouns would be repeated again and again. This would become awkward and confusing. Read the letter below from a camper named Cheryl to her parents. Replace each underlined noun or set of nouns with an appropriate pronoun. (The first one has been done for you.) Note that you may need to change some verb forms. Reread the letter to make sure your improvements make sense.

Dear Mom and Dad,

~~Mom and Dad~~ *You* were right. Camp is fun! Courtney and Cheryl have met kids from across the state. Most of the kids are friendly and nice to Courtney and Cheryl. Courtney and Cheryl hope to write to some of the kids and become pen pals when Courtney and Cheryl come home.

Courtney fell from a horse and sprained her ankle. Now Courtney cannot participate in any sports activities. Courtney says the crutches really are a pain. Cheryl thinks Courtney is having fun anyway, though.

Cheryl misses Mom and Dad, but Cheryl is glad Mom and Dad encouraged Cheryl to come.

Love,
Cheryl

Name _____ Action & Linking Verbs

Jumpin' Java

An **action verb** expresses physical action you can see or mental action you cannot see.
>Many Americans <u>drink</u> coffee.
>They <u>enjoy</u> the taste.

A **linking verb** expresses a state of being. It links the subject with a word or phrase that names or describes the subject.
>Coffee <u>was</u> popular years ago.
>It <u>remains</u> popular today.

Underline the verb in each sentence. Above each verb write A *for action verb or* L *for linking verb.*

1. A new coffee house, "Jumpin' Java," opened in our neighborhood.
2. It roasts its own coffee.
3. The specialty coffee and tea selections are wonderful.
4. I especially like cappuccino.
5. They also serve espresso.
6. The place also bakes its own sweets.
7. A glass case holds French pastries and cookies.
8. Patrons also eat biscotti there.
9. Biscotti are quite popular now.
10. The cafe offers live folk music on Thursday evenings.
11. Mike and I enjoyed the performance last week.
12. Friday night is comedy night there.
13. Professional and amateur comedians perform.
14. The place always seems crowded.
15. The coffee house attracts patrons to other neighborhood businesses, too.
16. We love it.

Name _____   Main & Helping Verbs

Lending a Helping Hand

A **verb phrase** consists of a main verb and one or more helping verbs. A helping verb helps the main verb make a statement or express an action.

Laura is looking for a new job.

(helping verb)   (main verb)

Some common helping verbs are *am, is, are, has, have, had, do, does, did, must, might, may, was, were, can, could, will, would, shall,* and *should.*

Read the following sentences from newspaper classified ads. Underline each verb phrase, then circle the helping verb(s).

1. Terrific Travel Company is seeking a detail-oriented individual for a secretarial position.

2. Wallpaper hangers are needed at the Milton Hotel in Mertzville.

3. A dynamic city brokerage firm must find a high-energy assistant.

4. Experienced window washers should apply in person.

5. Stiller's Supermarket may expand next year.

6. Exciting new company is looking for hard-working people.

7. A growing distributor of janitorial products must hire four warehouse persons.

8. A local car wash is expanding its business locations.

9. Two restaurant partners are selling their successful pizzeria.

10. Technical writing and training consultants will enjoy the atmosphere of Innovations Corporation.

11. An established national restaurant chain is offering franchise opportunities to qualified prospects.

12. A successful tennis racket manufacturer can establish you in the business.

13. One of Springfield's highly respected law firms is scheduling interviews for professional word processors with at least three years of experience.

14. A quickly expanding landscape company will need additional employees next spring.

15. A well-known bakery/restaurant will offer franchises to qualifying investors.

Name: _____   Principal Parts of Verbs

Silly Sentences

Every verb has four principal parts: present, present participle, past, and past participle. An auxiliary verb accompanies present participles and past participles. Present participles are formed by adding -ing to the present form. The past and past participle of most verbs are formed by adding -d or -ed to the present form. (Sometimes a spelling change is involved.) Some verbs form the various parts with new words.

Examples:

Present	Present Participle	Past	Past Participle
plan	planning	planned	planned
break	breaking	broke	broken

Fill in the missing forms of the verbs below.

	Present	Present Participle	Past	Past Participle
1.	_____	_____	*talked*	_____
2.	*run*	_____	_____	_____
3.	_____	*riding*	_____	_____
4.	_____	_____	_____	*wanted*
5.	_____	_____	*baked*	_____

Write four different sentences that could appear in the thought bubble for the cartoon below. Each should include a different principal part of a verb. For example, imagine a cartoon that shows a teenage girl with her finger stuck in a drain. Here are some possible thoughts she could have:

  Present tense: I <u>see</u> a problem here.
  Present participle: I hope no one else <u>is seeing</u> me do this.
  Past tense: I <u>saw</u> my contact lens down there.
  Past participle: I <u>have seen</u> better days.

Present tense: _____

Present participle: _____

Past tense: _____

Past participle: _____

©1998 McDONALD PUBLISHING CO.   9   PARTS OF SPEECH

Name _____   Simple Verb Tense

Yesterday, Today, and Tomorrow

There are three simple verb tenses.
    A verb in the **present tense** places the condition or action in the present.
        We study math after dinner.
    A verb in the **past tense** places the condition or action in the past. The past tense of regular verbs is formed by adding *-d* or *-ed*. (Sometimes a spelling change is involved.) The past tense of other verbs is formed with a new word.
        She liked my new hairstyle.
        I knew she would like it.
    A verb in the **future tense** places the condition or action in the future. It is usually formed by adding the helping verb *will*.
        The family members will come to the reunion.

Write the correct tense of the given verb in each of the following sentences.

1. Yesterday I (borrow, past) _____ my brother's radio without asking.
2. He (like, present) _____ to listen to music while he (wash, present) _____ the car.
3. When he (go, past) _____ to look for the radio, it (is, past) _____ not in his room.
4. He (is, past) _____ very angry with me.
5. He (tell, past) _____ Mom what I had done.
6. I (promise, past) _____ never to go in his room again without permission.
7. Today my mom (catch, past) _____ him taking my tennis racket.
8. He didn't even ask if I (need, past) _____ it!
9. Mom (talk, past) _____ to him, and I know he (remember, future) _____ to ask permission next time.
10. He (say, present) _____ we're even, and I (guess, present) _____ he's right.

Write three sentences about a living person you admire. Tell something about the person's past, about his or her life today, and about the person's future. Use the three simple verb tenses.

Present Tense: _____

Past Tense: _____

Future Tense: _____

©1998 McDONALD PUBLISHING CO.   PARTS OF SPEECH

Name _____   Perfect Verb Tense

Just Perfect!

There are three perfect verb tenses. Each tense is made up of a form of the verb *have* and the past participle.

The **present perfect** tense tells about an action that started in the past and is continuing or has just been completed.
   He <u>has seemed</u> nervous lately. Our class <u>has finished</u> the history test.

The **past perfect** tense tells about a condition or past action that was completed before another past action began.
   We <u>had driven</u> for two hours when we ran out of gas.

The **future perfect** tense tells about an action that will be completed before a specific time in the future.
   By the end of May <u>we will have read</u> five of Shakespeare's plays.

Write the correct tense of the given verb in each of the following sentences.

1. Mark (return, present perfect) _____ from his recent trip to Canada.
2. He and his family visited a cabin they (hear, past perfect) _____ about from friends.
3. Mark said that as soon as they arrived there his family realized they (make, past perfect) _____ a mistake.
4. The cabin was much more rustic than they (anticipate, past perfect) _____.
5. Mark told me that while he was there, he kept thinking to himself, "I can't believe I (spend, future perfect) _____ a whole week without electricity!"
6. The first night, just after Mark's family (go, past perfect) _____, to sleep, a bear tried to break in to the cabin.
7. The next day they went fishing. Just when they (drop, past perfect) _____ their lines into the water, they noticed the boat was sinking. They had to swim to shore.
8. When that happened, Mark said to himself, "All we need is a thunderstorm. Then this vacation (be, future perfect) _____ just perfect!"
9. Just then it started to rain. At that moment, Mark's entire family decided that their first wilderness trip (be, past perfect) _____ their last.

©1998 McDONALD PUBLISHING CO.   PARTS OF SPEECH

Name _____   Irregular Verbs

A New Home

Irregular verbs are verbs that do not follow rules when forming past tense and past participles. The chart below shows some examples of irregular verbs.

Verb	Past	Past Participle
be	was, were	been
wear	wore	worn
show	showed	shown
run	ran	run
see	saw	seen
catch	caught	caught
begin	began	begun

Write the correct verb tense for each irregular verb in the story below.

Last year, my family moved and I had to transfer to a new school. I (be, past tense) _____ not happy about this change, since I (be, past participle) _____ excited about starting high school in my old neighborhood with my friends. As the time (approach, past tense) _____ and my family (prepare, past tense) _____ for the move, I (become, past tense) _____ more and more nervous. Finally, it (be, past tense) _____ time to start our long journey to our new home. When we (arrive, past tense) _____ in our new neighborhood, I (begin, past tense) _____ to feel a little more at ease when I (see, past tense) _____ that there (be, past tense) _____ plenty of kids my age around. My first day of school, which I (dread, past participle) _____, really (be, past tense) _____ not bad at all. In fact, I (make, past tense) _____ quite a few friends right away. It sure (help, past tense) _____ that I (join, past tense) _____ several sports teams and clubs at school. Soon, I (begin, past tense) _____ to look forward to going to school and meeting new people. Even though I still (think, past tense) _____ about my old friends, I didn't miss them as much as I (have, past tense) _____ at the beginning. As I look back on the experience, I am glad that my family (decide, past tense) _____ a year ago to move here!

©1998 McDONALD PUBLISHING CO.   PARTS OF SPEECH

Name _____   Progressive Verb Tense

Making Progress

The progressive form of a verb expresses an action that is continuing. The progressive form of a verb is made up of a form of the verb *be* and the present participle.

Present progressive: *The students are working hard.*

Past progressive: *The students were working harder yesterday.*

Future progressive: *The students will be working hard tomorrow.*

Present perfect progressive: *The students have been working hard all day.*

Past perfect progressive: *The students had been working hard last week.*

Future perfect progressive: *The students will have been working hard for a week.*

Complete the chart by writing the six progressive forms for each of the verbs shown.

	1. talk	2. write	3. swim
Present Progressive			
Past Progressive			
Future Progressive			
Present Perfect Progressive			
Past Perfect Progressive			
Future Perfect Progressive			

Imagine your school has just received a national award. You and a group of students will travel to Washington, D.C., to receive the award in a special ceremony. Write the brief speech you will give to explain how your school won the award. Use at least three different progressive verb forms in your writing. Underline the progressive verb forms.

_____
_____
_____
_____
_____

Name _____   Transitive & Intransitive Verbs

Look for an Object

A **direct object** is a noun or pronoun that receives the action of the verb in a sentence. To find the direct object in a sentence, ask *what* or *whom* after the verb.

A **transitive verb** is a verb that has a direct object. It expresses action that passes from a doer (subject) to a receiver (direct object).

	Doer	Transitive Verb	Receiver
Mike saw a snake.	Mike	saw	snake

An **intransitive verb** does not have a direct object. The verb has a doer but no receiver.

	Doer	Intransitive Verb
Mike moved quickly away.	Mike	moved

Many verbs can be used with or without direct objects. They can be transitive in one sentence and intransitive in another.

Mike moved the box. (transitive)
Mike moved quickly. (intransitive)

Underline the verbs in the sentences below. Write T above each transitive verb and circle its direct object. Write I above each intransitive verb.

1. In his first game, the quarterback threw seven incomplete passes.

2. Monica slept through the night.

3. Tom, please move that box into the garage.

4. The frightened young boy called his mother's name loudly in the supermarket.

5. Tony climbed slowly into the tree house.

6. The man walked quickly to the post office.

7. The actors gathered behind the curtain.

8. I broke your new china.

9. No one hears your words.

10. The star hockey player gave the crowd quite a show last night.

11. Car sales increased last year.

A Change of Voice

A sentence can be written using either the active voice or the passive voice. To understand the difference between the two voices, examine the sentences below.

Susan played the piano.
This sentence is written in the active voice.
The subject *(Susan)* performs the action *(played)*.

The piano was played by Susan.
This sentence is written using the passive voice.
The subject *(piano)* receives the action *(being played)*.

Read the following sentences to determine whether they are written in the active or the passive voice. In each blank, write A *for* active voice *or* P *for* passive voice.

1. _____ The popcorn was eaten by the children.
2. _____ The bus driver parked near the zoo.
3. _____ The children lined up on the sidewalk.
4. _____ The children were given name tags.
5. _____ A tour guide spoke briefly with the teacher.

Underline the verbs written in the passive voice in the paragraph below. Rewrite the paragraph in the active voice.

    The seventh grade class was taken on a field trip to the zoo. The students were driven by one of the school's bus drivers. The Children's Zoo was toured by the students. There a newborn chimpanzee was seen by the group. The chimp was being fed a bottle by a zookeeper. The students were asked by the zookeeper to suggest names for the chimp. The students were told by the zookeeper that a membership to the zoo would be won by the student with the best suggestion.

_____
_____
_____
_____
_____
_____
_____
_____
_____

Name _____   Conjunctions

Putting It All Together

A **conjunction** joins words, phrases, or clauses in a sentence. **Coordinating conjunctions** connect words or groups of words that have the same function in a sentence. Some coordinating conjunctions are *and, but,* and *or.*
Julius <u>and</u> James are twins.
Julius likes math, <u>but</u> James likes science.

Correlative conjunctions are conjunctions used in pairs. Some correlative conjunctions are *both…and, either…or, neither…nor,* and *not only…but also.*
<u>Both</u> *Julius <u>and</u> James enjoy sports.*
<u>Either</u> *Julius <u>or</u> James will lead the band.*

Subordinating conjunctions join a main clause and a clause that depends on the main clause to make sense. Some subordinating conjunctions are *when, if, than, before, unless, although, after,* and *since.*

Add appropriate conjunctions to complete the sentences below.

1. The basketball player dribbled by his opponent, spun around, _____ made a three-point shot.

2. Many students wanted to finish their research papers early, _____ some students waited until the last minute.

3. I'll eat _____ soup _____ a sandwich for lunch today.

4. Susan will go to the movie _____ she does not have to work.

5. I think I'll have vanilla ice cream today, _____ I enjoy chocolate ice cream, too.

6. Don't horseplay in a crystal shop _____ you are prepared to pay for broken items.

7. _____ the waiter _____ the manager apologized for the poor service.

8. You can buy the movie tickets today _____ I paid last time.

9. I hope that someday I'll grow taller _____ Jason is.

10. My dad painted the walls, _____ my mom painted only the trim.

11. The teachers wanted to review the information with the class _____ she gave them the test.

©1998 McDONALD PUBLISHING CO.   PARTS OF SPEECH

Name _____   Conjunctions & Compounds

The More, the Merrier!

The **subject** of a sentence is who or what the sentence is about. Two or more subjects joined together are called a **compound subject**.

<u>Popcorn</u> and <u>candy</u> are available at the movie theater.

The **predicate** of a sentence is what is said about the subject. Some sentences have **compound predicates**.

The movie <u>played for two hours</u> and <u>ended at 8 o'clock</u>.

The words that join compound subjects or compound predicates are **conjunctions**.

Underline the compounds and circle the conjunctions in each of the following sentences. In each blank, write CS *if the sentence contains a compound subject,* CP *if it contains a compound predicate, or* B *if it contains both.*

1. Luke, Julie, and Laura wanted to go to the movies on Saturday. _____

2. They would see a science-fiction movie and eat pizza afterward. _____

3. Since Julie's parents were on a trip, Julie and Laura were staying together. _____

4. Laura and Luke called their mothers for permission and said they would be home by 9 P.M. _____

5. Karen and Mike overheard the telephone conversations. _____

6. They decided to join the group at the movie but knew they had to call home first. _____

7. Their parents gave them permission and told them to have fun. _____

8. The whole group drove in Luke's car and stopped at the bank for money first. _____

9. They arrived at the theater and learned that the science-fiction blockbuster was sold out. _____

10. Luke and Laura decided to see an action-adventure movie instead and bought two sodas and a large popcorn to share. _____

11. Mike, Karen, and Julie went on to dinner and said they'd pick up the others after the movie. _____

12. Laura and Luke enjoyed the movie and munched on their snacks. _____

©1998 McDONALD PUBLISHING CO.   17   PARTS OF SPEECH

Name _____ Interjections

Say It with Feeling

An **interjection** is a word or group of words that show emotion. Interjections are often punctuated with an exclamation point or separated from the rest of the sentence by a comma. Some common interjections are *oh no, ouch, whew, wow, hey, oh my goodness, oops,* and *hurray.*

Write an appropriate interjection for each situation below. Use correct punctuation.

1. _____ I won three million dollars!
2. _____ I can't believe you just knocked over Dad's new telescope.
3. _____ You've got to be kidding!
4. _____ Here are the car keys I've been looking for.
5. _____ That plate sure is hot.
6. _____ That test was easier than I thought!

Now write a sentence that might follow each of the interjections below.

7. Oops! _____
_____

8. Ouch! _____
_____

9. Aha! _____
_____

10. Yikes! _____
_____

11. Hooray! _____
_____

Some interjections were popular in the past but are not used as often today. Write the correct letters in the blanks to match these "old-fashioned" interjections with the emotions they expressed.

12. ____ Fiddlesticks!   A. Surprise
13. ____ Hot Dog!   B. Discovery
14. ____ Eureka!   C. Disappointment or frustration
15. ____ My Stars!   D. Excitement

©1998 McDONALD PUBLISHING CO.   PARTS OF SPEECH

Describe It to Me

An **adjective** is a word that modifies, or describes, a noun or pronoun. An adjective tells *what kind, how many,* or *which one(s).* *A, an*, and *the* are special adjectives called **articles**.

what kind: <u>mystery</u> novels
how many: <u>two</u> authors
which one(s): <u>those</u> books

Underline the adjectives in each of the following sentences. Circle the nouns they modify.

1. Mother bought a new Italian cookbook.
2. She tried a pasta recipe last night.
3. It was chicken cannelloni with a cream sauce.
4. She used leftover chicken from a previous meal.
5. It took a long time to prepare, but only ten minutes to bake.
6. The Mediterranean dish contains heavy cream and olive oil.

In the sentences above, the adjectives come before the nouns they modify. Sometimes, however, adjectives follow the nouns the modify. Adjectives that follow linking verbs are called **predicate adjectives**.

That book is <u>wonderful</u>.
Dennis always seems <u>impatient</u>.

Underline the predicate adjective in each sentence below. Circle the noun or pronoun it modifies.

7. The spaghetti Dad makes is fantastic.
8. Its taste is truly delicious.
9. The family recipe is secret, though.
10. Some parts are easy to figure out.
11. The noodles are store-bought.
12. The vegetables must be fresh.
13. The sauce, however, is mysterious.
14. Its taste is sweet, yet spicy.
15. Dad's cooking skill is really quite amazing.

Name _____ Adjectives

Typical Terms

An **adjective** is a word that modifies a noun or pronoun. An adjective tells *what kind, how many,* or *which one(s).*

Many adjectives can be identified by their suffixes. List three adjectives that end with the following suffixes.

1. -ful _____ _____ _____
2. -ish _____ _____ _____
3. -able _____ _____ _____
4. -y   _____ _____ _____
5. -less _____ _____ _____
6. -ous _____ _____ _____
7. -some _____ _____ _____

Many adjectives are overused. Brainstorm three adjectives that could replace each of the following overused adjectives.

8. pretty _____ _____ _____
9. little _____ _____ _____
10. funny _____ _____ _____
11. good   _____ _____ _____
12. big   _____ _____ _____
13. bad   _____ _____ _____

Adjectives can be very helpful in writing a description that appeals to the senses. Write a paragraph about something that appeals to one of your senses (sight, hearing, smell, taste, touch). Perhaps it is a food you enjoy or your favorite view. Be sure to include many descriptive adjectives in your paragraph.

_____
_____
_____
_____
_____
_____
_____
_____

©1998 McDONALD PUBLISHING CO.   PARTS OF SPEECH

Name _____ Possessive Adjectives

Children's Stories

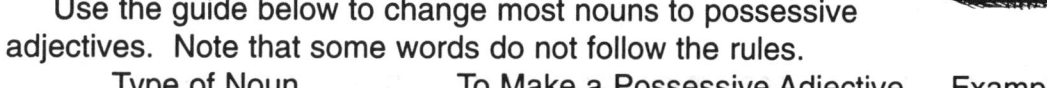

A **possessive adjective** shows who or what owns a thing or quality.

the book of a child — a <u>child's</u> book

Use the guide below to change most nouns to possessive adjectives. Note that some words do not follow the rules.

Type of Noun	To Make a Possessive Adjective	Example
a singular noun	Add *'s*.	tale — tale's
a plural noun that ends with *s*	Add *'*.	stories — stories'
a plural noun that doesn't end with *s*	Add *'s*.	children — children's

Rewrite each fairy tale phrase below so that it includes a possessive adjective. Identify the story each group of possessives refers to.

1. the magic of seeds _____
2. the melody of a harp _____
3. the wrath of a giant _____
4. the growth of a vine _____
5. the eggs of a goose _____

STORY: _____

6. the honesty of a mirror _____
7. the kiss of a prince _____
8. the work of small men _____
9. the trick of a queen _____
10. the poison of some apples _____

STORY: _____

11. the chime of a clock _____
12. the search of a prince _____
13. the taunting of sisters _____
14. the magic of a wand _____
15. the transformation of mice _____

STORY: _____

Now it's your turn. Write four phrases that refer to a well-known fairy tale. Each phrase should contain a possessive adjective.

1. _____   3. _____
2. _____   4. _____

STORY: _____

©1998 McDONALD PUBLISHING CO.   PARTS OF SPEECH

Name _____ Possessive Adjectives

Tricky Terms

Some students find that using the possessive adjectives *its* and *their* correctly can be rather tricky.

Its is a possessive adjective meaning "belonging to it."
It's is a contraction of "it is."

Their is a possessive adjective meaning "belonging to them."
There is an adjective meaning "in that place."
They're is a contraction of "they are."

Write its *or* it's *in each blank below.*

1. _____ fun to go to the zoo.
2. Summer visitors to a zoo are likely to discover that summer is _____ busy season.
3. Many people may be surprised to learn that _____ fun to visit a zoo in winter.
4. _____ true that some animals will be hibernating.
5. A groundhog, for example, may stay in _____ hole.
6. A polar bear, on the other hand, may be in _____ glory.
7. It may walk about, and play, and even swim in _____ pond.
8. Write a sentence containing the possessive adjective *its*. _____
_____

Write their, there, *or* they're *in each blank below.*

9. _____ go our new neighbors.
10. _____ very nice.
11. _____ new to this area.
12. I noticed that _____ license plate says Montana.
13. I have always wanted to go _____.
14. I have heard that _____ are beautiful mountains in Montana.
15. _____ tall and majestic.
16. Maybe I can go _____ next summer.
17. I'll ask my neighbors _____ opinion about places to visit.

©1998 McDONALD PUBLISHING CO. PARTS OF SPEECH

"Scent"sational

An **adverb** is a word that modifies a verb, an adjective, or another adverb.

She tries hard.
(Modifies the verb *tries*.)

The kitchen is very messy.
(Modifies the adjective *messy*.)

She cooks quite badly.
(Modifies the adverb *badly*.)

An adverb can answer the questions *how, when, where, how often, in what manner,* or *to what extent.* Many adverbs end in *-ly*. Some common adverbs appear in the box below.

quite	carefully	extremely	truly
finally	suddenly	really	especially
slowly	very	always	never
easily	quickly	almost	sometimes

Underline the adverb in each of the following sentences. Circle the word it modifies.

1. An animal's senses appropriately suit the animal's various needs.

2. Some animals have a very strong sense of smell.

3. Sharks can easily smell blood in the water from a distance of one hundred yards.

4. The smell of a poisoned shellfish instantly alerts an otter to danger.

5. Dogs have a very advanced sense of smell.

6. Some dogs have scent organs that are extremely sensitive.

7. A bloodhound can even detect microscopic pieces of skin.

8. Cove fish, which live in darkness, rely heavily on their sense of smell.

9. Frightened animals often leave a scent to warn others of danger.

10. Scientists believe smell is one of man's most important senses.

11. Humans, however, have a much less sharpened sense of smell.

12. When another sense is lost or diminished, however, a human's sense of smell can greatly improve.

Adverb Additions

An **adverb** is a word that modifies a verb, an adjective, or another adverb. An adverb can answer the questions *how, when, where, how often, in what manner,* or *to what extent.*

Adverbs can make writing more effective. Fill in each blank with an adverb in the two stories below. The adverbs you add to the first story should make it more suspenseful. The adverbs you add to the second story should make it more frantic.

It was a dark, stormy night. I walked _____ along the deserted street, hurrying to get home. As I passed under a large tree, I could hear an owl calling _____ in the night. The sound of a dog barking _____ caused me to look around _____. _____, a shadow appeared on the wall behind me. It grew longer and more frightening-looking, then it disappeared _____ around the corner. I shuddered and thought to myself, "When am I _____ going to get home? It seems like I've been walking along this street _____!" Just _____, the shadow reappeared, approaching me _____. I closed my eyes and feared the worst. Feeling a wet nose and a sloppy tongue on my face, I opened my eyes. _____, it turned out to be my dog Max.

When I awoke, I _____ looked over at the clock to see how much more time I had to sleep. _____ I realized I had _____ overslept. I _____ sprang from my bed, threw on my school clothes, and rushed into the kitchen. All was quiet. My parents must have _____ left for work. I _____ gulped down a bowl of cereal and hurried out of the house toward the bus stop. As I _____ rounded the corner, I _____ saw that the other students weren't there. Was I late? Panic set in! I _____ looked at my watch. I had time to spare. Had the bus come early? Was my watch wrong? _____ the answers occurred to me. It was Saturday!

Name _____   Degrees of Comparison

Designating Degree

Adverbs and adjectives have forms called degrees of comparison.

Positive degree does not compare anything; it simply makes a statement.
   (Adjective) *I am a good swimmer.*
   (Adverb) *Tim's team fought hard.*

Comparative degree compares two things. The comparative degree is often formed by adding *-er* to a word or by using the word *more*.
   (Adjective) *My sister is a better swimmer than I.*
   (Adverb) *Dave's team plays more frequently than Tim's.*

Superlative degree compares three or more things. The superlative degree is often formed by adding *-est* to a word or by using the word *most*.
   (Adjective) *My brother is the most talented swimmer in our family.*
   (Adverb) *Kim's team tried hardest.*

Some words change spellings when forming the three degrees.
   good, better, best

Complete the chart below by writing the missing degrees of comparison.

	Positive Degree	Comparative Degree	Superlative Degree
1.		worse	
2.			most smoothly
3.	often		
4.		more skillfully	
5.			tallest

Which season of the year is your favorite? Which is your least favorite? Write a paragraph in which you compare your favorite and your least favorite seasons. Use a variety of adjectives and adverbs to form degrees of comparison. Include at least two positive degrees, two comparative degrees, and two superlative degrees. Underline all degrees of comparison.

_____
_____
_____
_____
_____
_____
_____

Name _____   Prepositions

Up, Down, and All Around

A **preposition** is a word that shows the relationship of a noun or pronoun to another part of the sentence. A phrase that contains a preposition is called a **prepositional phrase**.

My science class is ⓘn the main hall.

Some common prepositions are listed in the box below.

about	before	down	into	through	above
behind	for	of	to	after	below
from	off	under	around	beside	in
on	up	at	by	inside	over

Write two sentences that contain prepositional phrases. Underline the prepositional phrases and circle the prepositions.

1. _____
   _____
2. _____
   _____

Many common expressions contain prepositional phrases. Complete each prepositional phrase below to write a common expression. The meaning of each expression is written in parentheses.

3. (He is likely to get in trouble.) He's walking on _____
4. (Forget it.) Go jump in _____
5. (Keep it a secret.) Keep it under _____
6. (She is not being realistic.) She has stars in _____
7. (You told a secret.) You let the cat out of _____

Imagine you are a pirate who has just buried a treasure chest. Write a paragraph that tells how to find the treasure chest. Your paragraph should include many prepositions and prepositional phrases. Underline the prepositional phrases and circle the prepositions.

_____
_____
_____
_____
_____
_____

©1998 McDONALD PUBLISHING CO.   PARTS OF SPEECH

Think of a Word

Fill in the blanks below by writing any word that is an example of the required part of speech.

1. past perfect verb - it _____
2. past perfect verb - they _____
3. common noun _____
4. adjective in the superlative degree of comparison _____
5. proper noun _____
6. adverb that answers the question *how* _____
7. adjective in the superlative degree of comparison _____
8. interjection _____
9. present tense verb - you _____
10. common noun _____
11. interjection _____
12. present tense verb - I _____
13. preposition _____
14. past tense verb - she _____
15. adverb that answers the question *how* _____
16. adverb that answers the question *how* _____
17. past tense verb - she _____
18. past tense verb - she _____
19. past perfect verb - it _____
20. past tense verb - it _____
21. preposition _____
22. common noun _____
23. adjective _____
24. common noun _____
25. interjection _____
26. adjective _____

Noun

?

Adjective

?

Verb

?

Adverb

Think of a Word (continued)

Copy the words you wrote on the previous page into the blanks below to create a silly story. Match each word with its number in the blank.

THE CAFETERIA ROMANCE

The 11:45 bell (1)_____, and students raced into the cafeteria to eat their lunch. Some students (2)_____ lunch bags from home, while others waited in line to get their (3)_____. It was the (4)_____ time of day at (5)_____ High School. Lucinda, a cheerleader, sat at a table with her friends Peggy and Christine. Lucinda spoke (6)_____, gazing at the handsome Chad from across the room. "Oh, isn't he the (7)_____?" she asked. "(8)_____!" said Peggy, "I'll bet you've said that at least twenty times today. Why don't you (9)_____ over and ask Chad out on a (10)_____?" Lucinda looked shocked. "(11)_____! I can't do that! What would I (12)_____?" Christine rolled her eyes and looked over (13)_____ Chad. "Maybe I should just call him over here." She (14)_____ to wave in Chad's direction. Just then, Chad saw her, stood up (15)_____, and (16)_____ began to cross the crowded cafeteria. Lucinda (17)_____ and tried to run away. Unfortunately, she (18)_____ into the table and spilled her drink all over herself. She toppled over, taking her tray with her. Food (19)_____ in the air and (20)_____ everywhere. Chad, Peggy, and Christine looked (21)_____ her in horror. All conversation in the (22)_____ stopped, and everyone turned to stare at Lucinda.

Just then, Lucinda awoke from a (23)_____ nightmare. Looking around her bedroom, she realized it had all been a (24)_____. "(25)_____! That would have been the most (26)_____ day of my life! I'm glad it didn't really happen!"

©1998 McDONALD PUBLISHING CO. 28 PARTS OF SPEECH